the new aga cook

No3 good food fast

Also in the series

Breakfast & Brunch

Cooking for Kids

Laura James

the new aga cook

No3 good food fast

Absolute Press

the new aga cook

First published in 2003

First published in the United Kingdom by
Absolute Press
Scarborough House, 29 James Street West, Bath, England BA1 IAS.
Tel: 44 (0) 1225 316013
Fax: 44 (0) 1225 445836
E-mail: office@absolutepress.co.uk
Website: www.absolutepress.co.uk

ISBN 1 904573 05 3

Photography: Andy Davis
Food styling: Penny Chambers

For Tim

without whom…

good food fast

menu

tv suppers

emergency entertaining

and to finish...

I don’t have hours to spend in the kitchen

intro

If I could have more of anything, it would definitely be time. More time to spend with my children, my husband, my friends and myself! As time is precious and food is divine, I think it's important to have a stack of recipes that allow you to cook something delicious in minutes.

This book is designed to offer just that. Simple dishes that can be cooked with the minimum of fuss, but still taste scrummy. I hate feeling so exhausted that I end up eating something that's a compromise. It's so unnecessary, particularly as good food can be so uplifting.

I passionately hate the idea of fashion in food. Anyone who lived through the eighties and has had the misfortune to look back on the decidedly dodgy haircuts and fashions of the time surely must agree. Food should be one of life's pleasures, not something with which we have a complicated relationship dictated by what's currently 'hip'.

Which is why I've included in this book recipes that I've been cooking since I was old enough to reach for a pan, alongside things I've recently discovered a taste for.

I'm not a chef, a home economist or someone who has studied the art of cooking. I'm a busy journalist with four adorable and demanding children and a husband I love to spend time

so we often eat things that take little time

with. Because of this (although I enjoy it immensely) I usually don't have hours to spend in the kitchen, so we often like to eat things that take little time to cook.

One of the biggest myths about the Aga is that you can only cook complicated dishes that take hours. This couldn't be further from the truth. Because the Aga's always ready you don't have to wait around for it to pre-heat. Instead, you can just throw the food in or on to it with the minimum of fuss.

Life in my house is completely unstructured, a far cry from my childhood when each day had its own dish. Because of this – and our remote location – people tend to drop in unexpectedly and stay for longer than they'd planned. I love it, but sometimes it throws us into chaos on the food front.

The shops here close early and the nearest Waitrose is a three-hour round trip. So I try to make sure I have a stock of basics in the pantry, fridge and freezer. The recipes here are chosen to reflect that.

Cooking should be stress-free and enjoyable. The recipes in this book are deliberately loose, easy and, above all else, achievable. I hope you enjoy them...

Laura James

Simple dishes that can be cooked with the

minimum of fuss, but which taste scrummy

store cupboard staples

If you have a well-stocked kitchen you'll always be able to throw together a meal in minutes and will never be without a snack. Here's my list of things I'm never without.

Lemons One of the cook's best friends. If you buy an un-waxed variety you can use the peel as well.

Herbs Rosemary, oregano, thyme, basil – whatever you like best. It's worthwhile buying growing herbs from the supermarket so you can plant them out in a tub. That way you`re unlikely to run out.

Ice cream Tastes fantastic, can jazz up even the dullest pudding and is perfect for midnight feasts!

Cheese Parmesan for quick and easy pasta dishes, Cheddar for sandwiches, Gruyère for potatoes and Baby Bell to eat with biscuits.

Stock Either home-made or, if you don't have the time or inclination, then Joubere make fresh beef, chicken, vegetable and fish stocks of the highest quality in easy tubs that can be frozen. Equally, Marigold Bouillon is well worth the space.

Dried pasta Available in the cheap-as-chips coloured varieties, as well as the posh squid ink sort. Perfect for TV suppers or as posh food with friends.

Rice Arborio for risotto, Spanish for paella and Basmati for everything else.

Passata Useful as a base for so many sauces.

Tinned tomatoes For sauces and quick soups.

Onions and garlic Vital for so many recipes and it's intensely irritating to run out of them.

Potatoes One of the most versatile vegetables and so comforting. Who can resist creamy mashed potato?

Bacon A packet of good bacon in the fridge can save a cook's day. Great for adding a little interest to basic pastas and tiny pieces fried until crisp can be sprinkled over lots of dishes. Plus, when you're exhausted what better than a bacon sandwich on thick white bread?

Butter, cream and milk Trust me, without these you're stuck!

Olive oil Good quality olive oil for frying, to drizzle over food and as the base for salad dressings.

Eggs Organic free-range eggs are perfect to provide a meal-in-minutes omelette or to have lightly boiled with soldiers when it's all too much.

Wine A glass of wine restores the spirits in a way no other drink can. Also good for cooking various things!

tv suppers

Unglamorous as they undoubtedly are, TV suppers are an enjoyable part of modern life. I love sitting – tray on lap, glass in hand – watching an episode of Sex and the City. The local pizza company used to be one of my Friends and Family numbers until I discovered the unadulterated pleasure of whipping up home-made TV suppers. While you won't find these dishes served in a trendy restaurant, they're utterly delicious and seriously cosseting…

aga fish and chips

Good fish and chips are unbeatable; bad fish and chips are utterly unbearable. The Aga is perfect for cooking Britain's favourite dish and you can even have it on a Sunday when the chippie's closed

8 large, floury potatoes
2 tablespoons of organic sunflower oil
225g (8 oz) of self-raising flour
Pinch of garlic powder
300ml (10 fl oz) of lager (ideally organic)
Salt and white pepper
4 haddock fillets

I remember being utterly staggered at how easy it is to make beer batter. Really, it's easier than pancakes.

Cut the potatoes into chips. Cover in a healthy sprinkling of sunflower oil and place on a baking tray on the floor of the roasting oven for 30-40 minutes. Set aside a couple of spoonfuls of flour and mix with the garlic powder. Mix the rest of the flour, lager, salt and pepper in a mixer. The batter should be thick and gloopy – if it feels too thin add some more flour. Dip the cod in the flour and then the batter. In a large frying pan, heat 1cm (1/2 in) of oil until it's smoking. Add the fish to the pan and cook for a few minutes until the batter turns golden. Carefully lift out the fish and place it on a baking sheet. Put it on the grid shelf on the third set of runners in the roasting oven and cook for a further 10-15 minutes.

Serves 4

This batter is perfect with the meatiness of the

haddock, but can be used with other fish

best-ever baked potatoes

This is barely a recipe, more a reminder of just how fab good baked potatoes can be and a few suggestions as to how they might be served

Prick the potatoes with a fork. Pop the potatoes on the grid shelf on the middle set of runners in the roasting oven. They'll take 60-90 minutes. When they're done take them out, cut them in half and worry the middle a little with a fork before smothering them in butter.

Pizza Spuds

My children like them topped like pizzas, with a little tomato purée, oregano and Mozzarella. Simply halve the potatoes, smear on the tomato purée, sprinkle on the herbs, pop on the cheese and stick the potatoes in a roasting tin in the roasting oven for about 7 minutes.

Tuna and Mayo

Mix a small tin of tuna with a dollop of mayonnaise and a good grind of pepper.

Soured Cream and Bacon Bits

Instead of butter, use soured cream with chopped chives. Fry small pieces of bacon in a little oil for a fab bacon bits topping.

Savoury Cheese

Pop grated Cheddar on top of the potato halves with a splash of Worcestershire sauce. Place them in a roasting tin and put them in the roasting oven (middle set of runners) for about 5 minutes or until the cheese starts to bubble and brown.

I can't eat these without thinking of Fireworks

Night. I can almost smell the sulphur in the air

home-made burger

I just love burgers. I realised how far my addiction had gone when, in a gorgeous Parisian restaurant with seriously luxurious food on the menu, I chose a burger from the children's section!

400g (14 oz) of organic minced beef
1 medium onion, finely chopped
1 egg
Large handful of fresh breadcrumbs
2 tablespoons of coriander, chopped
2 tablespoons of fresh chives, chopped
Tablespoon of tomato ketchup
Salt and ground black pepper

4 burger buns
4 large lettuce leaves
1 large tomato
4 slices of good Cheddar cheese

In a bowl, combine all the ingredients from the first set, adding the breadcrumbs as required. Mould the mixture into burger shapes – they can be as round or flat as you like.

Place the grill rack in the large roasting tin and put the burgers on top. Place it in the roasting oven on the third set of runners and cook for 20-25 minutes, according to your taste.

Cut the burger buns in half. Pop in the burger on top of the salad, add a slice of cheese and put the top on. Serve on their own or with chips.

Serves 4

A burger in a bun – my kind of haute cuisine!

unorthodox omelette

Omelette experts would probably baulk at this recipe, but it tastes great, takes minutes and shouldn't require any shopping. We often have it for lunch while we're working

Butter, for frying
4 eggs
1 tablespoon of double cream
2 tablespoons of chives, chopped
Salt and freshly ground black pepper
2 tablespoons of grated Cheddar

Heat the butter in a heavy pan on the simmering plate. Put the eggs into a bowl and gently worry them a bit. This is different to frantic beating or enthusiastic whisking; it's gentler and will stop the omelette tasting at all rubbery. Add the cream, chives, salt and pepper.

When the butter starts to foam, oosh it about a bit so it covers the entire base of the pan and pour in the egg mixture.

As the egg begins to set, gently prise the corners away from the side of the pan and sprinkle on the cheese, ensuring it covers the whole omelette. Continue cooking until the omelette is just about set – the underneath should be a slightly golden colour and the cheese melted.

Tip the pan and fold the omelette in half. If you're sharing it, cut it in half at this point and serve on to a plate with buttered bread and some salad.

Serves 1-2

Be gentle with your omelette mix – too much

beating can knock all the fluffiness out of it

The combination of Parmesan and black pepper

parmesan chicken

This chicken tastes so good and takes minutes to make. I love it with green beans and broccoli – it feels so virtuous!

8 tablespoons of freshly grated Parmesan
Pinch of black pepper
1 egg, beaten
4 skinned, boneless chicken breasts
Tablespoon of olive oil
Tablespoon of butter

Mix together the Parmesan and pepper. Brush the chicken breasts with the egg, then dip them in the Parmesan mixture.

Put the olive oil and the butter into a large, heavy-bottomed, oven-proof pan. Heat it on the boiling plate for a minute or so. Pop in the chicken, turning it after a minute or two, and then cook on the other side. Move the pan to the floor of the roasting oven and cook until it's ready, turning the chicken once. This will probably take 5-7 minutes, depending on the thickness of the chicken breasts.

You can serve with this with chips, potato salad, a crisp green salad or fine green beans and broccoli. Scrummy.

Serves 2-4

lend this dish a deliciously crisp finish

chicken and pepper pitta bread

You can, of course, fill pitta bread with anything you like, but I like it best like this. The onions caramelise beautifully and the chicken and peppers work particularly well together

Tablespoon of butter
Tablespoon of olive oil
1 large onion, chopped
1 red pepper, sliced
1 green pepper, sliced
1 yellow pepper, sliced
4 chicken breasts, sliced
4 pieces of pitta bread
Soured cream

Heat the butter and olive oil in a large, flat-bottomed pan on the simmering plate. Place the onions in the pan and cook for a few minutes. When the onions have started to caramelise, add the peppers and continue to cook for another 5 minutes. Toss in the chicken and stir it around so it gets covered in the pan juices.

Cook for a further 10-15 minutes, ensuring the chicken is cooked through.

Meanwhile, warm the pitta bread in the roasting oven for a minute or so. Cut it open and fill with the chicken and vegetables.

Top with the soured cream and enjoy!

Serves 4

sausages and mash in onion gravy

There are few things that conjure up childhood as effectively. The mash is the perfect foil to the richness of the sausages and gravy

Butter
6 plump sausages
2 medium onions
Tablespoon of flour
Half a glass of red wine
150ml (5 fl oz) of hot stock
6 large potatoes
Tablespoon of double cream
Freshly ground black pepper

Melt the butter in a roasting tin on the simmering plate. Add the sausages and let them cook gently, turning occasionally. Chop the onions and add them to the roasting tin. Transfer the tin to the second set of runners in the roasting oven. Leave them for about 15 minutes until the onions are soft and the sausages cooked.

While the sausages are cooking, peel the potatoes and cut them into quarters. Bring them to the boil in a large pan on the boiling plate. Remove the sausages and keep them warm at the back of the Aga or in the simmering oven. Transfer the tin to the simmering plate and add the flour. After a minute, add the red wine and stock. Allow it to bubble on the simmering plate, stirring occasionally until you have a thick gravy. Drain and mash the potatoes with some butter, the cream and pepper.

Serves 4

The creamy mash is in wonderful contrast to

the rich, savoury sausages and onion gravy

pasta with tomato sauce

When I left home I did so armed with my record collection, an assortment of questionable clothes and this recipe. While my taste in music and fashion has moved on, I still cook this all the time

2 400g (14 oz) tins of plum tomatoes
1 teaspoon of olive oil
1 clove of garlic, crushed
1 large onion, chopped
Half a teaspoon of sun-dried tomato purée
Half a glass of red wine
Small handful of fresh basil leaves, chopped
Maldon salt and freshly ground black pepper
1 packet of pasta of your choice
Freshly grated Parmesan

Heat the oil in a large pan on the simmering plate. Add the onion and garlic and cook until they're soft. Roughly chop the tomatoes and add them, their juice, the wine, the basil, tomato purée, salt and pepper to the pan and move to the boiling plate. Bring to the boil. Cover the pan and move it to the simmering oven for 20 minutes. Cook the pasta in a large pan of salted water. Drain the pasta and serve. Take the pan with the sauce out of the simmering oven and spoon the sauce over the pasta. Sprinkle with grated Parmesan and serve with garlic bread.

Serves 2-4

The ultimate fast-food dish… ready in moments

ridiculously easy pasta

Sometimes, after a hard day, all I want is a big bowl of comforting blandness. When my mouth hurts from smiling and I'm incapable of uttering another word, I crave this deliriously cosseting pasta dish

1 small packet of fresh spaghetti
1 clove of garlic, crushed
2 tablespoons of butter
4 rashers of bacon, chopped
Handful of freshly grated Parmesan
Black pepper

Bring a large pan of salted water to the boil on the boiling plate. Add the pasta and bring back to the boil. Move to the simmering plate and cook according to the manufacturer's instructions.

Melt the butter in a large pan on the boiling plate. Don't allow it to burn – just to froth nicely. Add the garlic and bacon and cook for a couple of minutes until the garlic is soft and the bacon is slightly crispy.

Take the pan off the heat. Drain the pasta and add it to the pan with the bacon and garlic. Stir it around so it becomes coated in the butter and bacon fat.

Add the Parmesan and put the pan back on the simmering plate for a minute or so.

Then add the black pepper and serve the pasta in large bowls.

Serves 2

and yet bursting with bright, natural flavours

pork with garlic and rosemary

It seems like an overstatement to call this a recipe. But the humble pork chop is often forgotten, so I see it as a reminder. They take minutes to cook and really are perfect for lazy nights in

1 large sprig of rosemary
2 large cloves of garlic
Maldon salt and a good grind of black pepper
Olive oil
1 teaspoon of crushed juniper berries
2 pork chops

Take the rosemary off the stalk and chop the garlic into tiny pieces. Add to a bowl along with the olive oil, juniper berries, salt and black pepper. Mix them together and then smear the mix over the chops.

Put a grill pan on the boiling plate and allow it to heat up for a minute or so. Place the chops in the pan. Cook them for two minutes or so, then turn them over and cook for another couple of minutes. Move the pan to the simmering plate and leave it there for about 5 minutes.

Turn the chops over to cook the other side for another five-or-so-minutes.

To check if they're done, make a small incision in the middle – if they're at all pink they're not done and should be left for a few more minutes.

Serves 2

emergency entertaining

There's no point getting frazzled over cooking dinner. Good friends don't expect Michelin-starred food, so you might as well whip up simple dishes that take minutes and can be prepared while you're chatting over a glass of wine

asparagus and parmesan risotto

The creamy consistency of the rice and the clean taste of the asparagus make this dish. Serve it with a bowl of salad and bread. Perfect on the sofa or as informal food for friends

Tablespoon of butter
1 onion, finely chopped
2 cloves of garlic, crushed
320g (11 $^1/_4$ oz) of Arborio rice
1 glass of dry white wine
1 litre of hot chicken or vegetable stock
1 tablespoon of butter
Freshly grated Parmesan

In a heavy bottomed oven-proof pan sauté the onion and garlic. Cook on the simmering plate for about 5 minutes.

Add the asparagus, then the rice and mix well until it's coated and cook until it's utterly transparent. Add the wine and stir until it's evaporated or been absorbed.

Move the pan to the boiling plate and add the stock and bring to the boil. Transfer it to the floor of the simmering oven and leave for around 20 minutes.

Check all the liquid has been absorbed and that the rice is tender and creamy, but still firm to the bite. Stir in the butter and Parmesan.

Serves 4

Totally ideal for cuddle-up evenings or when

a group of friends drop by unexpectedly

chicken with mozzarella wrapped in ham

This has a certain country house hotel kitsch, but tastes fab and is perfect when you've just got in from work and have friends to feed

2 balls of Mozzarella
4 skinned, boneless chicken breasts
8 slices of cured ham

I can't remember the first time I had ham and Mozzarella with chicken, but there's something about the combination that makes it truly wonderful. I first cooked it when I'd forgotten we had friends coming for dinner and it was an instant hit.

Slice the Mozzarella. Fry over the chicken until it's golden on both sides. Take it out of the pan and make an incision in the fleshiest part in the middle. Stuff the Mozzarella into the chicken and wrap slices of ham around each breast.

Transfer the chicken to an oven-proof dish and bake in the roasting oven, with the grid shelf on the lowest set of runners, for about 15 minutes.

Check the chicken is cooked through by cutting into it and making sure you can see no pink.

Serves 4

glazed steaks

If I'm feeling tired or stressed, all I crave is a seriously bloody steak and a huge plate of chips. The Aga is perfect – allowing the meat to sit in the simmering oven ensures it's beautifully butter-soft

4 tablespoons of toasted sesame oil
4 tablespoons of soy sauce
Salt and freshly ground black pepper
4 fillet steaks

Mix the sesame oil with the soy sauce, salt and pepper in a shallow bowl. Pop the steaks in and marinate for a few minutes.

Meanwhile, place a ridged grill pan on the boiling plate and allow it to get really hot. Place the steaks in the pan and allow them to cook for only a minute or so on each side. You want them to have lovely ridges from the pan, but not to get overdone in the slightest.

Remove the steaks from the pan, put them in an ovenproof dish and transfer them to the simmering oven for 5 or so minutes, depending on how you like them cooked.

Serve with a crisp salad in summer or a bowl of creamy mashed potato and fine green beans in the winter.

Serves 4

A really good steak is hard to beat… The Aga's

radiant heat positively locks in all the flavour

seared lamb fillets

Simple but effective, which is what emergency food is all about. You can't go wrong with this dish. It was one of the first things I cooked with an Aga and it shows how fab the simmering oven is

Tablespoon of sesame oil
4 thick lamb fillets
Salt and pepper

On the boiling plate, heat the oil in a large, heavy bottomed pan. Season the lamb fillets with the salt and pepper and place them in the pan. Leave them for about 5 minutes before turning them over and cooking the other side for the same amount of time.

Take the lamb out of the pan and put in an oven-proof dish. Place in the roasting oven for another 5-10 minutes, depending on how pink you like your lamb.

Cut into slices and arrange on warmed plates.

Serve with a big salad, creamy garlic potatoes (see page 49) and crusty bread.

Serves 4

Melt-in-the-mouth gorgeousness... The perfect

creamy garlicky potatoes

If I could only eat potatoes one way it would be like this. The soft potato swimming in garlic-infused cream is so divinely delicious it's difficult to imagine any potato dish surpassing it

1kg (2 $^1/_4$ lb) of potatoes
2 really fat cloves of garlic
Butter, to grease the dish
600ml (20 fl oz) of double cream
Salt and freshly ground black pepper

While this isn't the quickest dish to cook, it takes little preparation and needs only the most perfunctory of glances to make sure it's not browning too quickly. If it is, either cover the dish with foil – removing it for the last 10 minutes or so – or slide the cold plain shelf in above it.

Peel and thinly slice the potatoes. Slice the garlic. Grease the baking dish with a seriously generous amount of butter. Arrange the potatoes and garlic, in layers, in the dish, seasoning with the salt and pepper as you go along. Once they're all in, pour in the cream so that it almost covers the potatoes.

With the grid shelf on the floor of the roasting oven, slide in the dish and cook for between 1 and 1 $^1/_2$ hours.

Serves 2 as a main dish

accompaniment to any red meat or white fish...

swordfish with tomato and basil salad

Swordfish is best not messed around with too much. The meaty flesh of the fish tastes so yummy I prefer to cook it very simply

4 170g (6oz) swordfish steaks
Olive oil
Maldon salt and freshly ground black pepper
8 beef tomatoes
Handful of basil leaves

If you're cooking for friends and are in a hurry, this dish is perfect because it takes only about 10 minutes to prepare

Rub the swordfish steaks with a little olive oil and the salt and pepper. On the boiling plate, heat a ridged grill pan. When it's seriously hot, place the swordfish steaks in and cook for about 2 minutes on each side. Meanwhile, slice the tomatoes relatively thinly and arrange on the plates with the basil leaves. Drizzle over a little olive oil and grind some black pepper over them.

When the swordfish is cooked, serve it on the plates with the salad.

Serves 4

haddock with lemon and coriander

This tastes so clean and fresh that eating it makes one feel virtuous. There's something about good fish cooked well and treated simply that really brings out the taste of the sea

2 tablespoons of lemon rind, freshly-grated
2 tablespoons of flat-leaf parsley, chopped
2 tablespoons of coriander, chopped
Maldon salt and freshly ground black pepper
4 haddock fillets
Olive oil

I love buying fresh fish from my local fishmonger. Don't you find the colourful displays of the day's catch simply invite one to cook?

And don't be bashful about asking to inspect any fish you fancy – there should be no discernible odour and the eyes should be bright and vivid; not at all dull.

In a shallow bowl, mix together the lemon rind, parsley, coriander, olive oil, salt and pepper. Press each piece of fish into the mixture, ensuring it's well coated on both sides. Heat the olive oil in a large frying pan on the boiling plate. Cook the fish for a few minutes on each side, ensuring it's cooked through.

Serve with fresh vegetables and new potatoes.

Serves 4

scallops with pasta

Scallops are probably the easiest things to cook, but for some reason people imagine they'll be complicated. Because of this they always feel a bit posh and so are perfect as food for friends

1 large packet of tagliatelle
100g (3 $^{1}/_{2}$ oz) of butter
16 scallops
2 fat cloves of garlic, very finely chopped

On the boiling plate, bring a pan of water to the boil and put in the pasta. Bring back to the boil, move the pan to the simmering plate and cook the pasta according to the instructions on the packet.

Melt the butter in a large frying pan on the boiling plate until it starts to bubble. Add the garlic and cook for about 2 minutes. Then add the scallops to the pan and cook for a further 2 minutes. Turn over the scallops to cook on the other side for another couple of minutes.

Drain the pasta and put it on to warm plates. Top with the scallops, then pour over some of the garlicky butter sauce.

Serve with thick bread for mopping up.

Serves 4

This magical combination of colours and flavours

tiger prawn salad

Another dish that takes little time to prepare and is perfect for lazy summer suppers. My favourite evenings are spent in the garden chatting, drinking good wine and eating this kind of effortless salad

Salt and freshly ground black pepper
16 raw tiger prawns, shelled
100g (3 $^{1}/_{2}$ oz) of butter
2 fat cloves of garlic, very finely chopped
Large bag of salad leaves
2 large tomatoes, sliced
2 avocados
Salad dressing of your choice

Season the prawns with the salt and pepper. On the boiling plate, melt the butter in a large frying pan until it starts to bubble. Add the garlic and cook for 2 minutes, then add the prawns to the pan and cook for a further few minutes, stirring the prawns around. How long the prawns take depends on how plump they are. They're done when they have turned from grey to a glorious pink.

Arrange the salad leaves, tomatoes and avocado on plates and top with the just-cooked prawns. Pour over the dressing and enjoy!

Serves 4

would also work really well with scallops

lime and coriander prawns

Not a huge supper by any means, but perfect for summer evenings. You could, of course, serve this as a first course and have pasta or something to follow. But we usually have this and then a pudding

16 large tiger prawns
2 cloves of garlic, peeled and crushed
6 tablespoons of butter
1 tablespoon of coriander, finely chopped
Maldon salt and black pepper
5 limes

Peel the prawns, but leave the tails intact, then cut down the centre of each prawn and ease it open and remove the vein that runs down the middle. Open out each prawn and flatten it. Then rinse them under a cold tap.

Mix the butter, garlic and coriander in a bowl. Put the prawns in a roasting tin lined with Bake-O-Glide and smear on the butter mixture. Sprinkle with the salt and pepper and slide the roasting tin on to the middle set of runners in the roasting oven. Cook for about 6 minutes.

Put the prawns on plates and squeeze over a little lime juice.

Serve with lime wedges, fresh crusty bread and a bowl of crisp green salad.

Serves 4

Two beautiful flavours that together really sing

new potato salad

If you're called upon to provide food for friends, this potato salad is a great stand-by – we often have a bowl in the fridge and dip into it on an all too regular basis. It can be served warm or cold

500g (1 lb 2 oz) of Charlotte potatoes
3 large tablespoons of mayonnaise
Small bunch of spring onions, chopped
Salt and black pepper

Good potato salad is a real pleasure – the contrast between the waxy potato and the creamy mayonnaise is sublime.

You can add anything you like, of course – I like spring onions or chopped chives.

On the boiling plate, place the whole potatoes in a pan of cold salted water. Bring them to the boil and allow them to bubble away for 15-20 minutes until they're still firm and not falling apart, but are soft in the middle.

If necessary, chop the potatoes. Then put the potatoes in a bowl, add the mayonnaise, spring onions, salt and pepper and give it a good mix.

And that's it. Simple, but scrummy!

Makes 1 large bowl

details

Fish

FishWorks Direct delivers more than 24 types of fish, 10 varieties of shellfish and five smoked seafoods direct to the door. Call on 0800 0523717 or visit www.fishworks.co.uk

Meat

Donald Russell Direct offers truly wonderful meat which is vacuum-packed so it lasts longer in the fridge. Call 01467 629666 or visit the website at www.donaldrussell.com

Eggs

I can't stress enough the importance of using free-range organic eggs. For Freedom Farm Eggs, call Farmaround on 020 7627 8066.

Cheese

Neals Yard Dairy on 020 7240 5700 is one of the best places to get an extensive range.

Cookware

There are Aga Shops throughout the UK stocking a comprehensive range of cookware. They also host demonstrations and events. Call 08457 125207 to be directed to your nearest store.

Aga Magazine

A quarterly title with a 16-page recipe section in every issue. To subscribe, call 01562 734040.

Agalinks

Agalinks has a huge database of recipes from a host of chefs and cookery writers, including Mary Berry and Louise Walker. It's also home to the Aga Cookery Doctor, who will answer culinary questions and offer hints for successful cooking. Visit www.agalinks.com

Useful information no cook should be without...

thanks

I love this bit – it's my chance to gush! My thanks to...

Andy and Penny for such patience and creativity.

Everyone at Aga, Agalinks and Aga Magazine for their unfailing support.

Jon, Meg and Matt at Absolute for making me part of their team.

Dawn Roads – so knowledgeable and generous with her time.

Mary Berry and Lucy Young for being both inspirational and kind.

My family for putting up with my hissy fits and friends too numerous to name in turn.

Lastly, as ever, thank you to Tim – for everything.

Laura

Norfolk
Autumn 2003